To Jane & John

From a little author
To a BIG one —

Cass

THE PUBLISHING EXPERIENCE

Publications of the A. S. W. Rosenbach
Fellowship in Bibliography

John H. Powell, *The Books of a New Nation:
United States Government Publications,
1774-1814*

William Charvat, *Literary Publishing in
America: 1790-1850*

Curt F. Buhler, *The Fifteenth-Century Book*

Archer Taylor, *General Subject-Indexes
Since 1548*

Cass Canfield, *The Publishing Experience*

THE
PUBLISHING
EXPERIENCE

by
CASS
CANFIELD

A. S. W. Rosenbach Fellow
in Bibliography, 1968

PHILADELPHIA
UNIVERSITY OF PENNSYLVANIA PRESS

Grateful acknowledgment is made for
permission to use the letters in the
illustrative material.

CONTENTS

Introduction by J. W. Lippincott, Jr.   vii

I. The Real and the Ideal Editor   3

II. The Element of Chance: How Publishing   31
    Has Changed and Is Likely to Change

Afterword: Conversation with Leon Trotsky   57
    on February 4, 1940

Illustrative material   28

INTRODUCTION

In looking over the list of recipients of the A. S. W. Rosenbach Fellowship in Bibliography one might be surprised to find that 1968 is the first time since the Fellowship's establishment in 1930 that it has been awarded to a book publisher. It is, therefore, the first opportunity which the Friends of the University of Pennsylvania Libraries have had of listening to a lecturer from this industry discuss the important role a publisher plays in the bibliographic area.

It is particularly appropriate that the recipient of this Fellowship be Cass Canfield, Senior Editor of Harper & Row. For Mr. Canfield, in his forty-four years with the book publishing industry, spans a period which has witnessed some of the most significant and far-reaching alterations in the industry's long history. What he recalls in *The Publishing Experience* is only equaled by what he points out as the significant problems facing the industry today and by his forecasts for its future.

It was in 1924 that Mr. Canfield joined the firm of Harper & Brothers as manager of its London office, a position which had assumed major importance during Harper's first century of business because of the number and caliber of British authors the firm introduced to American readers. During his three years in London he was successful in bringing to the Harper list books by such important writers as Richard Hughes, E. M. Delafield, Philip Guedalla, J. B. Priestley, Harold Laski, Julian Huxley, and numerous others whose works are still widely read. Mr. Canfield returned in 1927 to Harper's main office in New York as assistant editor in the literary department and was elected a director of the firm. He became Executive Vice President in 1929, President in 1931 and Chairman of the Board of Directors in 1945. During all the years when he helped guide the management of this large and diversified company he was extremely active in Harper's general literature editorial program. He was instrumental in bringing to the Harper list books by an impressive roster of talented writers: Thornton Wilder, Louis Bromfield, John Gunther, Thomas Wolfe, and many other familiar names. It is as editor that he has been most widely known and respected.

In the summer of 1967 it was announced that Mr. Canfield was giving up his position on the Board of Directors but was continuing as the Senior Editor of Harper & Row and as Chairman of *Harper's Magazine.* Lest this announcement be interpreted in any way as an indication that he wished to become less involved in editorial matters, he addressed a letter to a number of his colleagues which *Publishers' Weekly* printed under the headline: "Cass Canfield Defines His Job."

> As Mark Twain observed about reports of his death, they were greatly exaggerated. So with rumors about my intention to ease up on my publishing work.

As recently announced, I am retiring from management duties and giving up my position as a member of the Board of Directors of Harper & Row, Publishers, which is being assumed by Cass Canfield, Jr. Actually, I've concerned myself for some time wholly with editorial matters and with dealing with the authors for whom I act as editor.

I have no desire or intention to cut down on my working schedule. It happens right now I'm involved with more editorial projects than at any time I can recall. So my future, for many years, is committed to present and potential Harper authors.

These were welcome words to those concerned about the growing trend away from the close author-editor association which had so distinguished American trade book publishing for more than a century and which appeared to be jeopardized in the structural changes brought about by mergers into companies outside the industry and by computers, mass distribution facilities, and competition from other areas of communications.

The Canfield lectures record a great era in the bibliographic field and mark a significant contribution to the area which Dr. Rosenbach chose to highlight by the creation of these Fellowships.

J. W. Lippincott, Jr.
Philadelphia

1

THE
REAL
AND THE
IDEAL
EDITOR

It is standard practice for a speaker to announce formally that he feels honored to have been invited to make an address. This produces a problem for me for I'm really at a loss to convey to you the extent of my appreciation for the invitation from President Harnwell to be the Rosenbach Fellow in Bibliography and, as such, to deliver two lectures.

I am fortunate in having met Dr. Rosenbach on several occasions. He was a great friend of E. V. Lucas, the English author and man of letters, whom I knew quite intimately. To be in Dr. Rosenbach's company was a delight; he combined scholarship with charm, and communicated to his friends his wonderful zest for life.

Just the other day I learned from my son-in-law, Joseph Fox, that his grandfather of the same name had encountered young Rosenbach at a small book auction in Philadelphia in 1895. Mr. Fox wanted to acquire a sixteenth-century manuscript-missal which he expected to buy for the proverbial song, but he had not counted on the presence of a young stranger, Rosenbach, then a college student. The bidding was brisk and Fox acquired the item, bidding higher than his competitor could afford. He noticed Rosenbach's crestfallen look and gave him a ride home in his victoria. As they conversed, Fox became more and more impressed with his companion; from this encounter developed a lifelong friendship. Joseph Fox provided the funds for setting up the Rosenbach business and so a great career as a book collector and dealer was launched. Those of you who have read the interesting biography of A. S. Rosenbach by Edwin Wolf and John F. Fleming may recall a brief reference to this incident.

I intend to discuss the publishing experience, which is nearly as old as the hills. Publishing far antedated the invention of printing. Under the Ptolemies, staffs of scribes prepared editions of the classics. In the Rome of the Caesars, slaves toiled to produce editions of books, and in the Dark Ages monkish copyists succeeded them. As Allan Nevins has described, a cloudy line of publishers stretches back from Mainz on the Rhine and Subiaco on the fork of the Tiber, the little towns whence printing first spread slowly over Europe. Some of the great publishing houses of today, like Longmans Green in London, date back to the eighteenth century.

If the value of my own publishing experience were measured in terms of time it could be called vast, comprising as it does 44 years with Harper, which was established in 1817, two years after the Battle of Waterloo. However, the value of experience should be related to the intelligence of the experiencer rather than to the mere passage of time. In fact the time element should be heavily discounted, for a perceptive person of thirty will have profited more from his mistakes than a plodder of twice his age.

In any case the value of experience is finite. While it's probably too extreme to observe, as did Earl Wilson, that experience is what makes you recognize a mistake when you make it again, the fresh, imaginative outlook is what means most in publishing. Taking the risk of making a mistake is essential to creative publishing.

Now I am primarily a trade publisher and editor; I shall use these terms interchangeably. My observations are mainly within that framework, although for quite a number of years I was chief executive of a publishing business — The House of Harper — comprising books in every field, including medicine, excepting only law books and reference volumes produced in sets. A trade publisher can be defined as one who caters to the general public which buys books in bookstores, as distinct from the buyers of books in special fields, like medicine, or textbooks.

In a piece I wrote for *Harper's Magazine* last year, I reviewed the history of the Harper firm over a century and a half in an attempt to discover what could be learned from it. I found, to my discouragement, that the publishing mistakes of the nineteenth century of overproduction and competitive price cutting were repeated in the twentieth, and that the editorial techniques of another age offered only limited guidance.

Furthermore, I must admit that after a great many years in the publishing business I still have little more idea of what kinds of books sell than I did when I started. I've pored over the sales records of titles we have published over the past twenty-five years and am still unable to produce meaningful generalizations about the necessary ingredients of a best seller.

What I have been saying is negative. Let me be

5

my insistence that he sign a contract before doing so—until a little alarm clock which he carries inside of him announced that the time had come to take the plunge and work on *Inside Europe*. The book appeared at just the right moment of crisis when Hitler and Mussolini were riding high and were laying their plans to conquer the Western world. The little alarm clock has served Gunther well over the years; in book after book he has covered areas of the world that were, at the time of his writing about them, at the explosive and critical stage.

The capacity for getting on with authors is, of course, essential to successful editing. They are a special breed; I was made to realize this at a dinner given for me in London by E. V. Lucas many years ago. He had invited about thirty men involved in the various arts and I found myself sitting next to Max Beerbohm. Since I knew only five or six of the guests I asked my neighbor to tell me something about the others and what they did. Beerbohm offered me a challenge; he said, "Look around the table and you can identify the writers. You'll find that they are the worried-looking ones; the painters, architects and sculptors appear, and are, relatively cheerful." I did as I was told, and, sure enough, correctly spotted the writers by observing their harassed expressions.

The business of the writer is, indeed, demanding and wearing—to a greater degree than the more instinctive occupations of painters or sculptors. The writer needs special attention and an editor who

8

understands him. This assignment for the editor is difficult, but has its own rewards because sometimes the editor is in touch with genius.

Among the most gifted writers I have known was J. B. S. Haldane, the English geneticist. He took no advanced degree at Cambridge but was blessed with an original mind. I remember his saying to me once, "I get one or two ideas a year. If you can achieve that, you're pretty well ahead of the game and of most people in science." His interest was research; he cared little for making his ideas known to the general public. But going into London on the train from the country he would become bored and start to scribble. These scribbles were published, several volumes of them. They have not been surpassed in grace of style and in scientific interest for the layman.

Such a man needs a sympathetic editor, as do most talented writers. Each one requires personal attention, a sensitive understanding of his or her particular problems. Awareness of this is essential for anyone working with authors.

Stories of other authors come to mind—Aldous Huxley and Edna St. Vincent Millay. Huxley was a strange and wonderful person. Perhaps the quality of his endlessly searching mind is best suggested by a story about him told to me by his older brother, Julian, the scientist. Julian related to me that Aldous, as a small child, was often lost in thought. One time, at the age of five, he was sitting by his mother, apparently oblivious of his surroundings. His mother asked him what he was thinking about, whereupon the child looked up, paused a moment, and said, "Skin." A most surprising line of inquiry for a five-year-old!

Edna St. Vincent Millay was one of the most extraordinary people I have ever known, combining a beautiful lyrical gift with the mind of a mathematician. She was professional to her finger tips, and took justified pride in the technical perfection of manuscripts she sent to us, her publishers. Although I should have known better, I once questioned her use of a classical phrase. Then all hell broke loose; after an avalanche of magnificently outraged letters from her, I caved in, properly chastised.

After her charming husband, Eugen Boissevain, died, she fell ill and was confined in the Doctors Hospital in New York in a very depressed state of mind. The question then arose as to whether or not she should be allowed to return to her home in Austerlitz, New York, as she wished to do. Her doctor sidestepped making a decision since there was a danger that in her melancholy condition she might commit suicide. So the decision was left to a few intimate friends, who were divided in their opinions, with the result that it was finally put up to her editor. I decided that she should be allowed to do what she wished and took her back to Austerlitz. On this rather long motor ride we confined our conversation to what we saw and observed on the way; when I left her in her lonely house I remember that she thanked me for my detachment and said, "I'm not going to kill myself. Don't worry." She didn't,

10

and lived for several years to write some very fine poetry.

To try to understand and help people of talent is difficult and rather wearing; needless to say, one often fails to satisfy them. Still, there are times when authors express to their editors extravagant and unwarranted appreciation. Dr. Alexis Carrel was a case in point. His book, *Man, the Unknown*, achieved outstanding success, not because of any brilliant promotion effort on our part but because we had reluctantly permitted a condensation of the work in *The Reader's Digest* which aroused wide attention. As a result the book took off and we could not keep it in print. Actually, we deserved a reprimand from the author. Instead, Carrel told me at the time, in his office at the Rockefeller Institute, that if scientists could plan and develop their programs with the foresight and accuracy we had shown they would achieve results beyond their wildest dreams. I listened to this dissertation, was grateful for the undeserved tribute and kept my own counsel.

The question is often asked whether the book publisher should seek to influence public opinion. Some publishers have done so, and succeeded, like Victor Gollancz in England, who represented the responsible Left. My own view, however, is that the publisher's primary role is rather that of the catalyst, to provide the means for the expression of any responsible opinion. His basic function, I think, should be to draw out his authors, to stimulate them so far as he can.

11

Occasionally one succeeds. I remember sitting next to Margaret Leech at a dinner party. We were strangers to one another but I knew of her as the author of some good novels. I found her extraordinarily intelligent. In the course of our conversation I developed a theory about historical writing, that the shorter the period covered, the more interesting would be the resulting book. I maintained that it was almost impossible to write a readable volume dealing with the whole development of Western civilization because in such a book events and personalities could not be described vividly and at sufficient length to hold the reader's interest. The conversation ended with my suggesting to her that she write a book covering only a fortnight in the life of Abraham Lincoln, which would give her the opportunity of reporting what was appearing in the press at the time, what Lincoln said to various important contemporaries, what people were thinking at a crucial period. The idea intrigued Miss Leech so that she prepared an outline. Actually it failed to satisfy her and she turned to another subject. But she kept to the concept of limiting the size of her historical canvas so that she could write about events in detail and describe what happened from day to day. She decided to write about the Civil War as it affected civilians in one locality—Washington, D.C. The book, *Reveille in Washington,* won the Pulitzer Prize and is still widely read today.

To what extent this work started a new trend in historical writing it is hard to say. The fact is that in succeeding years many arresting books of what I call concentrated history have appeared, like Jim Bishop's *The Day Lincoln Was Shot,* Walter Lord's *Day of Infamy* and his *Incredible Victory.*

So I emphasize that the role of the editor should be to try and stimulate his authors, to draw them out, rather than to attempt to impose his own ideas. Of course some degree of knowledge is useful to the editor and this helped me in working with Sumner Welles when he was writing *The Time for Decision* in the early months of 1944. My associate, Marguerite Hoyle, and I spent many days with Welles, asking him questions based on what we knew of recent international events. When Welles had reached the point in his book where he was to deal with the future of Germany, we asked him, "What are you going to propose? One Germany, two Germanys, or several Germanys?" To our amazement, since Welles as Under Secretary of State was primarily responsible for developing our postwar policy and had been working on this for many months previously, the reply was that he had not yet decided how to answer these questions. Two weeks later, when we saw him again, he had reached his conclusions and wrote the chapters on Germany. The pattern he proposed was substantially the one that was adopted in the postwar settlements. It can be maintained that in that fortnight the fate of Germany was determined.

I have spoken of the usefulness of *some* knowledge but would observe that too much may handicap the editor. Some years ago I visited Oxford, intent on finding a biographer for Elizabeth I of England. Had I known, as I should have, that an excellent biography of Elizabeth, highly regarded by scholars, was still in print I would not have bothered Hugh Trevor-Roper and A. L. Rowse by bringing up the subject, which they both dismissed at once. Nevertheless, we had interesting conversations and I knew just enough about the general period of Elizabeth to hold up my end. These conversations led to others, and as a result of that trip to Oxford, I acquired for the Harper list these two outstanding historians.

What the editor needs most is a nose like a hound, so that he can ferret out the best manuscripts submitted to him. The number of manuscripts that come to a large publishing house, thousands each year, is so great that the editor cannot possibly read them all. Consequently, he must rely on readers to a considerable extent and be able to evaluate their reports shrewdly through his awareness of his readers' tastes, prejudices, and fields of competence.

In most cases opinions on manuscripts are obtained from readers within the firm, but when an expert opinion on a given subject is called for, the editor approaches an outside scholar. A curious case, in this connection, occurred in the early 20's when the noted historian, James Harvey Robinson, was asked to read a hefty manuscript, obviously one of distinction. In due course Robinson's report came in, stating that while the book was of outstanding importance, it demanded so much knowl-

14

edge on the part of the reader as to be out of bounds for a commercial publisher. The book, which was declined by Harper, was Spengler's *Decline of the West,* not only a seminal work but one that has been in steady demand for several decades and will continue to be so for many more. The lesson is clear. The editor was right in accepting the expert's opinion on the value of the manuscript but should have ignored his views about salability, which he was not competent to judge.

The editor's evaluation of reports is a complicated business, as is the selection of readers. Some publishers establish rules, which I suspect, like the automatic declination of a manuscript which has failed to get an expert's approval. I doubt the wisdom of this kind of routine process because I feel that the editor must be the final judge about publication. It is up to him to decide whether a given expert's opinion may be prejudiced or may express too technical a view. For example, the manuscript in question might be a biography designed for popular consumption. Although such a book should be factually accurate it cannot, in its nature, be too inclusive nor encompass all the detail and all the sources a certain type of scholar might demand.

We're getting into a forest here, with no clear demarcations between light and shade, where, in my opinion, the only guide to follow is the wise editor, assuming he can be found. In this connection the editor in the Oxford University Press who spotted Rachel Carson's talent deserves a high mark. She was almost unknown at the time, a civil

15

servant in the Department of the Interior who had written only one book, for another publisher, *Under the Sea Wind,* which had been a publishing failure. This editor was absorbed by a manuscript that came in from Rachel Carson and so certain about its distinction and quality that he contracted for it immediately, ignoring the fate of her previous book. The manuscript was *The Sea Around Us,* a book that will, I believe, still be read as a classic when all of us in this audience have disappeared from the scene.

Occasionally a complete amateur may propose to the editor the right solution to a publishing problem. When Harry Hopkins died, having completed only his notes for writing an autobiography, we were faced with the problem of finding a writer for the book. His widow, Louise, the agent Brandt, and I spent hours conferring without result. The professionals in this group, Carl and Carol Brandt and I, suggested many candidates but none seemed just right. At a second meeting, when Louise Hopkins suggested Robert Sherwood, the pros shook their heads; we recognized Sherwood's great talent as a playwright but pointed out that he had never written an important book of nonfiction, let alone a biography. But Mrs. Hopkins pressed her point and we finally decided to sound out Sherwood, who promptly accepted the challenge. Her suggestion proved brilliant; after three years of work Sherwood produced a perfect manuscript that required no editing. The book, *Roosevelt and Hopkins,* was as fine as any that came out of World War II.

16

Once, another amateur, Charlie, a taxi driver, gave me a good publishing idea. He was feeling exhausted, having spent some hours at home trying to keep his large brood of young children amused. As we chugged along a country road in the taxi, he told me about his wearing experience and exclaimed, "I wish someone would write a book describing a thousand ways to amuse a child!" This despairing remark ignited a spark in my publisher-oriented mind so that I could say to him at once that the words he had uttered would yield him $100.00 from Harper. He was mystified until I explained to him that it was our custom to pay that sum to anyone who suggested an idea for a book project which we accepted. After that taxi ride the two of us parted happily and in due course Harper published *838 Ways to Amuse a Child,* by June Johnson, a successful book that sold over many years. Apparently many people share Charlie's frustrations with children and need help.

To reminisce is probably an indulgence but I take comfort from Santayana's observation: "Those who cannot remember the past are condemned to repeat it." The danger is to succumb to the temptation of emphasizing one's successes and glossing over the failures. Now I can assure you that the list of my mistakes is impressive, and venture the opinion that a thriving publishing business could be established on the foundation of the books turned down over the years by any large trade publisher.

Without doubt the majority of mistakes are made when the editor has to accept or reject a project

17

without benefit of reading a manuscript. There are times when a reading is impossible because the editor is called upon to make a decision regarding publication on the basis of an outline, sometimes on the basis of only a title and the author's name. As bidding for potential big sellers becomes more and more frantic this kind of situation occurs more and more frequently. There have been cases where up to a million dollars have been guaranteed to a famous political figure for his memoirs, without any opportunity for the book and magazine publishers to see a line of copy. Even when a good manuscript is submitted, the editor may fail to read it, having wrongly accepted negative reports from his readers, particularly at a time when his desk is piled high with manuscripts. Such experiences haunt the editor throughout his career, especially when he tosses in his bed in the grim early hours of the morning.

The need to give prompt decisions is another contributing factor to making mistakes. The desk of my predecessor, Eugene Saxton, would often sag under the weight of manuscripts he had read; he would explain this by observing that he had to allow several days after reading a book for it to sink in. When, after a week or so, he found that the scenes and characters of a novel were still vivid in his mind he would accept the manuscript; if not, he would decline.

Analysis of the mistake-making process could fill a five-foot shelf. The editor must resist the temptation to be awed by the great name, the powerful personality. On many occasions I've succumbed, but I do look back with amused pride on an episode of the 20's in my youth when I was in London.

The work day had started in an ordinary manner and I was looking forward to a rather grand party my wife and I were giving that evening for an American couple who had invited the Prince of Wales. An overseas call from a Paris agent, William A. Bradley, abruptly broke up my routine since I decided at once to fly to the Continent the same afternoon, abandoning my social responsibilities. The trip seemed very important because Bradley had informed me that the great Georges Clemenceau, the tiger of France, who had led his country to victory in the First World War, had just finished a book about the struggle between Athens and Sparta, designed to illustrate various aspects of the conflict between the French and the Germans. It was a way, he said, for him to express certain views about the great war which he felt he could not do except by "indirection."

On the following morning I was ushered into Clemenceau's presence; he really did have a tiger-ish look. Although I could read French readily, my conversational ability was limited; still, I had no difficulty in understanding the points he made. As the first American or British publisher to see his manuscript, of which he possessed only one copy, I was told to read it downstairs in his sitting room and to return with my report. He obviously expected a large offer.

Shaking with nervous anticipation, I shut my-

19

self in and started to read the book. It was prose in the grand manner. I found Clemenceau's ornate French style soporific and his allusions to World War I both hard to grasp and remote. There was no smell here of an American best seller, at least to my nostrils.

I was, of course, greatly disappointed, yet the fear of meeting Clemenceau's piercing eyes on my return to his study was my dominant reaction. How could I handle the situation? Well, I didn't; I stammered and mumbled, somehow managing to make my escape without having actually said no, and, certainly, without having said yes. I ran down the stairs, breathing hard and feeling free as air.

Clemenceau's book on the Greek struggle was eventually published in the U. S. It attracted little attention, so that I had fortunately guessed rightly. I was lucky to have avoided this publishing pitfall but will never forget the ordeal of having to face up to one of the most powerful, dominating figures of our time.

A publisher-editor may be judged in large part on how well he discharges his basic responsibilities in certain critical areas.

He must see that his authors' books are attractively produced, that they are effectively promoted and that they are well distributed. In my time the format of American books has improved considerably; for this, publishers owe a debt to Alfred Knopf, the pioneer in the field. I would say that book advertising techniques have also improved, although publishers continue to be faced with the problem of devising a distinctive advertising approach for each of the dozens of different titles they bring out each season, a challenge which most other manufacturers do not have to meet to anything like the same degree.

It is in the area of distribution that the original publisher of clothbound books has failed to make much progress. Here he must depend on wholesalers and retailers over whom he has little influence, unless he owns a bookstore or a chain of stores. But such ownership is necessarily limited in scope in view of the size of the country and the big network of bookstores needed to serve the American public. Quite recently new chains of bookstores have been started by merchandising concerns; these are often placed in suburban supermarket areas. They give some promise of better retail book distribution in the years to come.

Second, the editor stands or falls on his ability to persuade his authors to accept the changes and revisions he proposes to them or makes himself. Over and over again, particularly when an editor lacks tact, the author will leave him and seek a more sympathetic publisher. In many such cases the author will finally make the changes proposed by his original editor who started the process of softening up his resistance. In this circumstance the original editor may derive some melancholy satisfaction from having helped to improve a manuscript even though in the process he has lost an author.

To continue with the woes of the editor, it often

happens that, in an effort to keep his author, he will compromise on the revisions he thinks should be made. Then, when the book is published, the reviewers are likely to observe that, had the editor taken the trouble to do his job properly, it might have been worth space on a bookshelf.

Imagine the difficulties Max Perkins of Scribner must have had with Thomas Wolfe. Perkins slaved over Wolfe's massive manuscripts, helped to give them shape and contributed greatly to his author's stature as a novelist. Wolfe did for many years appreciate his editor's work; his relationship with Perkins was close; but in the end he left Scribner, feeling that he needed to assert his independence as a writer.

Thirdly, the publisher-editor must stand up for the interests of his author and defend him in a crisis. The obvious example that comes to mind is that of William Manchester's *The Death of a President*. The publication of this book involved endless complications, and the essence of the problem was whether the publisher would accept the stipulations of the Kennedy family or those of the author. The publisher was caught between Scylla and Charybdis; neither side would yield, and there was a good deal to be said for the very strongly held views of each of the parties. To have given in to the family was a temptation for many reasons, one of them our regard for the Kennedys. But that would have violated what I feel must be part of the publisher's ethic, that he defend the right of his author to express himself as he chooses. In this editorial battle

22

no one emerged the clear victor. Some compromises, not essential ones, were made with the result that nobody was completely satisfied. Nevertheless, the author's interest was defended; the result was a book which essentially reflected his opinions and observations and bore the imprint of his personality.

Another measuring stick for the publisher is the degree to which he fulfills his responsibility as a citizen. There are times when the publication of a book may be harmful to the interests of the country, when the editor must choose between his obligation to the author and the public welfare.

This kind of dilemma occurred when we published Leon Trotsky's biography of Stalin, a book that took many years in its preparation.

Early in 1940, when my wife and I were in Mexico City on vacation, it occurred to us that we should call on Trotsky, who was living there in exile. We arranged an appointment and, after penetrating several echelons of guards, which I quite wrongly felt were unnecessary window dressing, were finally ushered into his study. In the course of talking to this highly intelligent, charming, and thoroughly dangerous character I noticed a line of hooks on the wall behind his desk from which were hung galley proofs of the first half of his biography of Stalin. Trotsky was affable and interesting; he assured me that before many months had passed he would have completed the biography of his hated rival.

He never finished the book, for within a few

23

months of our visit he was murdered. In the struggle with his assailant, Trotsky was pinned against those hooks; his blood was spattered over the proofs, which were sent to our office in due course. They now rest in the Harvard College Library, covered with tragic brown stains.

The next step for us, Trotsky's publishers, was to find a qualified person to finish the book from the voluminous notes left by the author. We chose Charles Malamuth, a Russian scholar, for this assignment, which he performed very well, explaining in a preface exactly how the biography had been prepared. At last, after years of work, the book was produced and sent to reviewers on a Friday morning. I breathed a sigh of relief.

The final chapter of this story is concerned with what happened forty-eight hours later, on Sunday morning, December 7, 1941. Along with millions of fellow Americans, I heard on that day the terrible news of Pearl Harbor. After the first shock I began to think about the publishing problem presented by Trotsky's *Stalin*. It was obvious that, within a few days, Stalin would be America's ally and that he would not only deeply resent the appearance of this biography by his arch rival, but would never believe it possible that in the United States freedom of the press could reach the point where the government would, in such circumstances, permit publication.

Thus the publisher was caught between his contractual obligation to the author (in this case his estate) and what he felt was his duty as a citizen in wartime. I consulted three men I knew in Washington, each of whom had access to the President. They were evasive, observing that as Harper was a private enterprise it was entirely up to me, as editor of the book, to make up my mind whether or not to stop its publication. By Monday noon, after discussion with my associates, I had decided to withdraw the book. Our entire edition was placed under seal in our warehouse and held there for five long years by which time — it was then 1946 — relations between the United States and Stalin's Russia had deteriorated to the point where any obstacle to publication had been removed. So we then proceeded to publish at once.

Whether or not I did the right thing in the Trotsky case is debatable. I failed to live up to our publishing contract and set myself up as an arbiter of what was in the national interest without any instructions from our government. However, in my view, the editor-publisher must be willing to assume many kinds and degrees of responsibility. In doing so he is bound to make mistakes, but not as many as by evading responsibility.

The good editor-publisher is hard to find since he must be a person who combines qualities that do not often go together. He needs both a business sense and editorial acumen, with a gambling streak thrown in. In addition, he must possess a strong acquisitive instinct, although this should not be exposed to the surface. And finally, persistence is essential to the mixture, for when the editor gets an idea he believes in he ought to press it

25

hard, up to the point of irritating his author. Otherwise many good books would never be written since they frequently take shape many years after the projects for them were first discussed.

A requirement for an editor is a nose not only for manuscripts but also for people, for creative individuals who have not yet proved themselves as writers but who have in them the capacity to produce good literary work. This instinct is important because it so often happens that for lack of it an editor fails to hold an author of talent. An example of this was the case of Peter Matthiessen, a youngish author who writes distinguished fiction and books on nature subjects. Some years ago my firm published his promising first novel with moderate success. But when the second one was submitted, we considered it inferior to the first and advised the author to put it aside, with the usual result; he took it to another publisher.

We had used bad judgment, because if an editor believes in his author as a creative person, likely in the long run to produce significant writing, he should be prepared to take on one book, maybe several, about which he has doubts. The editor must gamble, basically, on his judgment of the author as an artist, rather than reach a publishing decision on a particular manuscript. This is what Alfred Knopf did as a young man when he worked for Doubleday. Knopf believed in Joseph Conrad, insisting that Conrad would one day be acclaimed as a great novelist, although his early books failed to achieve public acceptance.

26

I have made the perfect editor — the ideal all of us in publishing strive to attain — sound important and have meant to do so. He is indeed important, but he should remain the catalyst. For the great book can be produced by only one person, the man who writes it. The editor can sometimes suggest and provide a spark, he can help and support the writer. But he is and must continue to be the anonymous, and sometimes essential, man behind the scenes. His only monument can be the publishing house where he has worked.

3276 Deronda Dr
L A 28
Cal
August 30th 1956

Dear Cass

I have just heard from someone who has seen an advance copy that there is a 35¢ edition of _The Genius & the Goddess_ on the market. Is this so? I don't remember your telling me of it Also my informant tells me that it has a cover representing a young lady putting on (or taking off) her drawers!

I hope _tomorrow & T. & T._ is getting under way satisfactorily. Incidentally, how did _Heaven & Hell_ make out?

I expect to be in NY for a few days from Oct 10th & hope to see you then

Yours
A Huxley.

The late Aldous Huxley expresses qualified approval of a lady in underclothes.

November 14, 1941.

Dear Cass:-

     I like Gerald Johnson's book much --
and when I have finished reading it I am going
to get him to come to Washington to argue with
me about one or two estimates he makes, not of
me, but of some of my predecessors in the
Presidency! I think Gerald Johnson has done
the best possible job any contemporary could
do. In another fifty years my memory will be
in Heaven or Hell, one way or the other!

     As ever yours,

Franklin D Roosevelt

Cass Canfield, Esq.,
President, Harper & Brothers,
49 East 33rd Street,
New York, N. Y.

F.D.R.'s comments on *Roosevelt: Dictator or Democrat?* by
Gerald Johnson, published by Harper.

THE
NEW YORKER
No. 25 WEST 43RD STREET
NEW YORK, 36, N. Y.

EDITORIAL OFFICES
OXFORD 5-1414

September 11, 1964

Dear Cass:

     The prospects for a Perennial One Man's Meat
are inviting, and Katharine has agreed to introduce
it into her perennial border with the hollyphlox
and the acrimony. Instead of a royalty of 10% of
the wholesale price less 42%, I have been turning
over in my mind the idea of a 42% royalty but
without cross-fertilization, less ten of the little
ones. This would be the equivalent (if my mathematics
are right) of six long ones, if they're the size I
think they are. I am accepting your offer assuming.
I mean, I can't not go along with anything that is as
exciting and challenging as this except.

                           Yrs,

                                Andy

P.S. I saw Zane Grey on the street the other day. He
     looked awful.

Mr. Cass Canfield
Harper & Row
49 East 33rd Street
New York 16, New York

E. B. White's whimsical reply to a proposal for putting _One
Man's Meat_ into Harper's Perennial paperback line. The
postscript is his way of commenting on the continued post-
humous publication of Zane Grey novels.

31

Dec 8, 1964

50 DEEPWOOD DRIVE

HAMDEN, CONNECTICUT 06517

Dear Cass:

Many Thanks for your letter.

Yes, it's coming on; the end is in sight.

I didn't foresee so long a work and I'm a little wonderingly amused that I've flagged so seldom — had so few and so short intervals of discouragement and doubt. My father used to wring his hands over what he feared was my "lack of perseverence".

Long sections are now coming back to me from the Typist.

I still don't know how it "ends", — how the plot-lines converge and express the ideas that govern the book. Gertrude Stein used to say that you should always leave a portion "open" —— don't work too close to a determined <u>schema</u> : if you've built correctly the material itself will dictate its culmination.

I talk of it as being long, but it won't be a long book compared to many others — merely the longest I ever ventured upon.

There's a good deal of painful matter in the book — it's about how we variously confront, endure, assimilate, evade, or accept the tragic circumstances in life, but there are some very funny passages, too. and I like to think that Cass will as much approve the one aspect as he will enjoy the other.

As I draw to its close I must remove myself from civilization again. I leave soon to spend Christmas day with an aged aunt in Florida .... then take a slow ship to Europe (Curaçao to Genoa), then soon after take another slow one back. There's nothing like a tight little, right little cabin, rocked in the cradle of the waves, to work in.

A MERRY CHRISTMAS

Happy New Year

Your old friend

Thornton

A progress report on *The Eighth Day* from Thornton Wilder.

Edna St. Vincent Millay, accompanied by the author, receiving an honorary degree at New York University in 1938.

34

Presentation by the author to Eleanor Roosevelt of a copy of
This Is My Story, the first volume of her memoirs. Henry
Hoyns, onetime president of Harper, in background.

West Cornwall
Connecticut
May 2, 1960

Mr. Cass Canfield
Harper & Bros.
49 East 33rd Street
New York, New York

Dear Cass:

I agree with you that one publisher from now on is
the best thing, and it still leaves me with a total of
four. Others keep calling up, too. I think maybe we
should proceed one book at a time though, and I don't
know which I will finish first, "The Nightinghoul" or
a new collection of stories and essays, tentatively
called "Lanterns and Lances". I have about fifteen
pieces finished for it and should finish five more
this spring and early summer. That ought to bring it
above sixty thousand words.

Planned publisherhood is not the easiest thing in
the world, as you know. It's like planned parenthood -
you can never tell what's going to happen between covers.

Our best to you and all the rest.

As ever,

Jim Thurber

JT/ew

James Thurber's response to Harper's expression of interest
in his future books after publication of *Alarms and Diversions*.

Cass C. J·B·P. K·F·C

The Good Companions
New York
Feb. 1931

Drawing by J. B. Priestley on endpaper of his novel *The Good Companions:* Priestley in the center, flanked by the author and his wife. Priestley's inscription reads, "The Good Companions in New York."

Dear Cass Canfield:

It occurs to me with something of dismay, that, if I were dead---instead of being, as I am, alive and kicking, and I said kicking --the firm of Harper & Brothers (Est 1817---and how good is your Latin?) might conceivably, acting upon the advise of a respected **friend, alter one word in one of my poems.

This you must never do. Any changes which might profitably be made in any of my poems, were either made by me, before I permitted them to be published, or must be made, if made at all, someday by me. Only I, who know what I mean to say, and how I want to say it, am competent to deal with such matters. Many of my poems, of course, are greatly reduced in stature from the majesty which I hoped they might achieve, because I was unable, as one too often is to make the poem rise up to my conception of it. However, the faults as well as the virtues of this poetry, are my own; and no other person, could possibly lay hands upon any poem of mine in order to correct some real or imagined error without harming the poem more seriously than any faulty execution of my own could possible have done. (I do not, of course include here such hastily-written and hot-headed pieces as are contained in "Make Bright the Arrows", "the Murder of Lidice", etc. I am speaking of poetry composed with no other design than that of making as good a poem as one possibly can make, of poetry written with deliberation and under the sharp eye of an ever-alert self-criticism, of poetry in other words, written with no ulterior motive such as, for instance, the winning of a world-war to keep democracy alive)

As for sonnet XlV from "Epitaph for the Race of Man", let me assure you now (because I know that you are deeply troubled about this matter and in a mood to accept from a friend whose learning you respect, a

38

2.

suggested alteration in one of my poems) let me assure you that your best friend has brashly leaped to an ill-considered conclusion, and that in this instance he has made a complete ass of himself.

This particular sonnet is guilty of a serious fault, but from the point of view of sonnet-structure, not from the point of view of either fact or mythology. The octave is written in the pure Italian form, whereas in the sestet the rhyme-scheme (ssided) is improper. This is very bad, of course. Yet I do consider this particular bastard sestet to be sometimes as in this sonnet, for instance, not ineffective.

As to what this sonnet actually says,- well, it seems to me that any bright boy in the eighth grade, who cared for poetry, and was not too lazy to look up a few words in the dictionary, would have little difficulty as to its literal meaning. If this poem makes any statement at all, which it does, than the substitution of the word "Ixion" for the word "Aeolus" would render the whole sonnet utterly ridiculous, confusing and meaningless......

I would not, if I were you, in the future, pay much attention to any suggestion made to you by this acquaintance of yours on the subject of poetry, for which, it would seem, he really cares little, and concerning which, even more seriously, he knows even less. He is not, in any case, a thorough going student: he is a pouncer upon details and his scholarship - if indeed it exist al all - is bumpy and uneven.

Sincerely yours, and with every good wish for the New Year,

Edna St. Vincent Millay

January 8th, 1946.

Edna St. Vincent Millay, writing in 1946, declares in no uncertain terms her exclusive right to correct her own work.

39

Adlai Stevenson and Albert Schweitzer, whose books Harper published.

The late Louis Bromfield at Malabar Farm, Ohio. The author
was his friend and publisher over many years.

Four and five hundred
dollars per article are being
paid by other magazines for
what I am asked to do at $20 or
$15 a thousand words! No
provision is to be made for my
return — none for my expenses.
The policy of compulsion
not only oversnaps itself in
the end; but during the time
it can operate it only results
in paralyzing creative ability,
and disgusting a man with
his employers. That a man should
work three years without any return
for his labor except promises,
necessarily destroys all confidence in
any promises, & money itself at last
ceases to be a consideration —

Lafcadio Hearn

Sometimes the relation between an author and his publisher leaves much to be desired, as this letter from Lafcadio
Hearn, written in the last century, indicates.

2

THE
ELEMENT
OF
CHANCE:
HOW PUBLISHING HAS CHANGED AND
IS LIKELY TO CHANGE

The element of chance in trade publishing is less than in poker and about the same as in baseball. Much, of course, depends on how skillfully the editor uses the breaks that come his way, but occasionally a plum falls into his lap without any real effort on his part.

This was the case with Thomas Wolfe. In the late 30's I happened to encounter Bernard DeVoto at some literary function and was surprised when he said to me that he understood that Wolfe, having decided to leave Scribner for the reason described in my previous lecture, had been calling someone in our firm. I rushed back to the office to make inquiries but came up against what seemed a blank wall. It took me quite a time to get any response other than vacant stares. Finally one editor told me that a man calling himself Tom Wolfe had telephoned from long distance. But, he explained, it couldn't have been Wolfe because the talk was extremely rambling and the man on the wire sounded like someone under the influence of liquor. So the editor, tired of a conversation with a person he felt was an impostor, rang off.

Well, it *was* Wolfe, understandably in an agitated state, and there was not a moment to lose. I did the obvious thing. After making sure that Wolfe's decision to leave Scribner was irrevocable, I got hold of him and his agent immediately and arranged for the publication of his succeeding books. The first one we published was *The Web and the Rock*. This fine novel and those that followed added

45

great prestige as well as profit to our firm over many years—a result due entirely to that chance meeting with DeVoto.

The acquisition of Thornton Wilder for the Harper list occurred because one day, shortly after his *The Bridge of San Luis Rey* had been published with critical acclaim, but before it had become a best seller, I made up a list of eight or ten promising novelists and asked my secretary to send them our circular announcing the Harper Prize Novel contest, with my business card enclosed.

I never really expected to hear from any of them and so was quite taken aback when young Wilder came in to see me. He asked questions about the contest, thanked me for giving the answers and thereupon departed rather hurriedly. Since he had said nothing about sending us a manuscript I assumed that this was the end of the matter.

To my surprise Wilder telephoned me a couple of weeks later and suggested that I look him up if I should happen sometime to be in the neighborhood of Lawrenceville School, near Princeton, where he was teaching. I found it difficult to hold off making the trip even for an hour and, after allowing a decent interval of a couple of days to elapse, showed up at the school.

We talked many hours. It developed that at the moment Wilder had received the Harper Prize Novel announcement, he was thinking about which publisher he would choose to bring out his future work, having decided to leave Albert and Charles Boni, the publishers of *The Bridge*. We got on well

46

then as we have ever since, so that he decided to cast his lot with Harper. The continuing connection with Thornton Wilder has been a source of deep satisfaction to me; I was particularly proud and pleased to publish *The Eighth Day* in 1967, forty years after the appearance of *The Bridge*.

Good fortune like that which attended me in the case of Wilder was also the lot of Alfred Harcourt not long after he and Donald Brace had started their firm on a very modest financial basis. The partners were faced with the need of building up a list of authors, so that when Harcourt returned from a scouting trip to London in 1918 Brace asked him anxiously what he had been able to find. Harcourt replied that, unfortunately, the leading British authors were signed up with other publishers but admitted that he'd picked up an interesting book on economics and a promising one of historical essays, information that hardly thrilled his partner, who was thinking of bigger fish. But these "little" books turned out all right, the first being Keynes' *Economic Consequences of the Peace*, the second, Strachey's *Eminent Victorians*. At about the same time Harcourt Brace published Sinclair Lewis' *Main Street*. The new firm was made, "wiv a little bit o' luck" combined with editorial acumen.

To continue in this cheerful vein, I can cite an example where not only luck was involved but also alcohol, which triumphed over bad judgment. This occurred at the time I was employed by our firm in London. With the certainty of youth I had various fixed opinions, among them that an essayist could

47

not be expected to write successful fiction. Accordingly, when my friend and contemporary, the agent A. D. Peters, suggested that I commission J. B. Priestley to write a novel, paying a modest advance of a hundred pounds, I refused, explaining that I would have to see a manuscript before making an offer. Peters, no older but wiser, suggested a meeting with Priestley in a Fleet Street tavern. It was a delightful occasion. As we enjoyed lively talk we consumed, between us, nine pink gins. The atmosphere changed and, by the time we parted company, the idea of refusing to pay a paltry hundred pounds for Priestley's novel struck me as absurd. A deal was made, and not long after, his famous book, *The Good Companions,* became a well-deserved fiction best seller on both sides of the Atlantic. Priestley has remained a close, lifetime friend, and we look forward next year to publishing his account of the turbulent, extravagant Regency period.

The break is what the trade publisher is always waiting for, like the racetrack enthusiast. One followed my seeing a startling photograph in *Life* a few years after World War II. This showed a shark coming head on toward a man equipped with a device of which I had then never heard, an Aqualung. As I gazed at this picture it occurred to me that the diver, whom the caption identified as Jacques-Yves Cousteau, might possibly be persuaded to write a book. I acted on the impulse and got in touch with our agent in Paris, with the result that in due course Cousteau's *The Silent World,* edited by my associate, Evan Thomas, was pub-

48

lished with considerable éclat in many countries throughout the world.

A current break is Stephen Birmingham's *"Our Crowd."* Although we anticipated a good sale for this book we didn't expect a runaway. The same thing happened with George Plimpton's *Paper Lion* the year previous. Such successes, unexpected in scale, are what keep the trade editor's sanity when his favorite books are spurned by the critics and the public.

The good breaks are pleasant to remember; they offset the dismal periods when the pursuit of the wanted authors and books produces no results, when the competing publishers seem to pluck all the choice fruits. It has happened to me on scouting trips to London, after three weeks of an exhausting series of calls on agents and publishers, after a succession of lunches, dinners, and cocktail encounters, that nothing of any real value or interest has turned up. In these circumstances one is apt to take on a book or two in desperation, in a misjudged effort to justify the trip.

In contrast, occasionally the dice *can* fall exactly right. Not long ago I took the shuttle to Washington, after the office day, in order to get the advice of a well-known Catholic writer as to who might be induced to travel around the world and write a book about the Church in many different countries, analyzing the opposing views and the conflicts within the Catholic organization. Although I had not previously known this writer we established a good rapport and discussed the project with mounting

49

enthusiasm, with the result that he accepted the assignment himself. His book should be completed within the next year.

Having made this satisfying arrangement, it occurred to me later that evening that I might call on my friend Stewart Alsop. I had the feeling that the time had come when I might persuade him to write a book despite the demands of his journalistic work. I pointed out to him that his twenty-year experience as a very successful Washington correspondent had given him a unique perspective for writing about the politics and personalities of the capital. By 1:00 A.M. he had, to my delight, agreed. His book, *The Center: People and Power in Political Washington,* was a well-deserved success.

That was, indeed, a fruitful trip.

Not long ago, I had another lucky evening. I was about to leave the office late one afternoon to take a plane to South America when the phone rang and my friend and distinguished lawyer, General Edward Greenbaum, with whom I had worked closely on the William Manchester affair, asked to see me. When I inquired whether the matter was urgent, explaining my imminent departure, he allowed that it was. So we met, with Evan Thomas, neither of us having the slightest idea of what was on his mind.

It turned out that General Greenbaum had arrived from Europe only half an hour before our meeting, and that he had been talking with Svetlana Alliluyeva in Switzerland about her book, *Twenty Letters to a Friend.* He explained that her

50

situation was so delicate and complicated as to require his making arrangements at once, and secretly, for American publication. He named the large sum that was required and emphasized the necessity for an immediate decision.

Thomas and I were electrified; we were fascinated by Greenbaum's account of Svetlana's escape and by all the circumstances surrounding this famous episode. The question was: How could we commit the firm to a large guarantee on the basis of an hour's conversation without any firsthand knowledge of what her book contained? We resolved the matter by telling the General that if we could obtain two good reports on the Russian manuscript within the next few days we would proceed enthusiastically with the publication plan he proposed. The reports were received shortly so that, as I was flying around the Peruvian mountains, I received the happy news from Thomas that the deal had been made.

Being a person of cheerful disposition, I have emphasized the good breaks rather than the bad ones. But if you have been given the impression that a publisher can rely on his luck, I have misled you, for chance provides no solid foundation for a publishing enterprise. In fact, ways must be found to minimize the gambling element in this business, particularly the trade end of it.

One way is for the editor to be on the constant lookout for quality, because any book of quality, except for one on a highly specialized subject, finds its audience and is apt to continue in demand for years. In 1929 I conceived the idea of a twenty-volume history of modern Europe from the Middle Ages to the present, to be written by American scholars. I approached William L. Langer, then head of the history department at Harvard; he agreed to be the editor of the series and within a matter of months we had signed up most of the authors we wanted. It was a rather bold experiment at the time because the books were designed for the general reader, rather than as textbooks. In fact my friend Alfred Harcourt, who was considerably my senior, warned me that the books would be unsuccessful, that they would fall between two stools. There was the danger that the public at large would find them too difficult and that college teachers would not think them suitable for their requirements. In that era there was a considerably greater gap than today between the textbook and the serious nontextbook.

As things have turned out the series has done very well. All the volumes which have been published are still in print and they continue to sell year after year in both clothbound and paperback form. Certainly this is an example of long-term publishing since half a dozen of the volumes are still uncompleted. Langer remains as the editor and is fulfilling his function as brilliantly as when he started on the enterprise.

Encouraged by the success of *The Rise of Modern Europe,* I persuaded Professors Henry Steele Commager and Richard B. Morris to act as editors of *The New American Nation Series,* to consist of over forty volumes, of which more than half have been published over recent years. These books, too, have received wider acceptance than we expected, particularly from the general public.

Long-term sellers bring cheer to the harassed publisher. It is always a pleasure for me to think of Donnelly's *Atlantis,* which remained in print for 82 years. In another field, I was cheerfully surprised to note the other day a new printing of E. B. White's delightful children's book *Charlotte's Web* — fifty thousand copies, bringing total copies in print (clothbound) to 700,000.

The question is often asked whether a trade publisher can minimize his risk by following the trends of public demand. I am doubtful about this guideline; besides, I believe that generally it is the fresh and the unexpected that appeal to the reading public. In the period between the two world wars it became a cliché in publishing circles that memoirs by Russian émigrés were failures; one after another had been published with dismal results. So we editors felt that we had found at least one safe rule to follow: to decline Russian memoirs. We turned our minds to other subjects, at least until *The Education of a Princess* by Grand Duchess Marie hit the best-seller list, where it remained a long time. Another rule had been shattered because an author had appeared who could write freshly and interestingly about an experience which others had described in wooden prose.

I recently read an article on Thornton Wilder by Richard H. Goldstone and was struck by a passage which confirms my doubts about the predictability of public taste in terms of trends. It reads:

> While *The Cabala* had been about aristocratic life in contemporary Rome, Wilder's new novel with an eighteenth-century Peruvian setting — all about love but without a love story — was as unlikely a contender for the best seller lists of 1927 as anything that boomtime America could conceive. It was the year that serious readers were buying Sinclair Lewis's *Elmer Gantry,* Dreiser's *The Financier,* and Hemingway's *Men Without Women.* That is to say, realistic-naturalistic fiction was secure in the saddle. But for reasons that have been analyzed yet never explained, Wilder's *The Bridge of San Luis Rey* sold well over a quarter of a million copies in its first year of publication. It also catapulted an obscure and astonished young author into international celebrity.*

In the course of this discussion of chance in trade publishing I've come up with only one safeguard for the editor: to look for quality. It is a good one, and intelligent application of the quality precept leads to the acquisition of worthwhile books. However, I believe that the good trade editor should also be capable of finding books that meet the demand of the big reading public for entertainment. This editorial function is to my mind more difficult than that of spotting literary quality.

*"The Wilder 'Image'" in *four quarters,* May, 1967.

How can an editor judge the public taste with any accuracy? My answer is that he cannot; it defies analysis. In my opinion, when the editor chooses a book because he figures that it will appeal to a large popular audience, he usually guesses wrong. The only answer to this problem is that the editor needs to have the same kind of mind—the reactions—of the mass audience. What interests and amuses that audience must be what interests and amuses him. Let me give an example: When Harold Latham of the Macmillan Company accepted with enthusiasm Margaret Mitchell's *Gone With the Wind,* he did so not because he had analyzed the public taste but because he was carried away with this wonderful story and was sufficiently representative of the average reader that he picked a great best seller.

Another case that comes to mind is that of Betty Smith. She had submitted to one of our editors, Elizabeth Lawrence, a manuscript for a nonfiction contest then sponsored by the firm. Miss Lawrence was touched by its human quality but felt that it did not come off as a memoir. Accordingly, she advised the author to fictionalize her experience. The result, after much work and excellent cooperation between author and editor, was *A Tree Grows in Brooklyn,* another famous best-selling novel. Again, the editor's identification with the public's taste was the determining factor in the choice of the book; Elizabeth Lawrence's emotional reaction was that of the typical reader.

Sometimes the public taste for fiction is very

55

"corny," sometimes it is not. The superior editor chooses those popular books which have some merit for the simple reason that they are the ones that appeal to him. That kind of editor would be useless to a publisher seeking the highly sensational, meretricious type of best seller which has appealed to a part of the mass audience since the inception of American publishing.

In fact, it must be admitted that some pretty awful reading matter achieves a large following; also that some cheap publishing tricks are effective. When mass paperbacks were started in this country nearly thirty years ago, the publishers used the public opinion polling organizations to determine the type of jackets that would move these books off the racks. I recall one series of rather distinguished novels which failed to sell; among them was Robert Nathan's *One More Spring,* a charming story of a love affair set in New York's Central Park. It had an attractive picture jacket in good but not highbrow taste. The services of the poll experts were used to determine what kind of jacket would appeal to the mass paperback audience and thereupon a new, lurid one was produced showing a girl and boy snuggling up on a park bench. Result: *One More Spring,* up to that time a paperback dud, started to sell at a very brisk pace. In this connection I would point out that a substantial part of the mass audience for paperbacks is the same as that for the pulp magazines of another day; its buying habits are peculiar. This audience has bought tens of thousands of copies of *The Art of*

Loving, Erich Fromm's excellent psychological analysis of human behavior, thinking, no doubt, that they were getting some pretty hot stuff.

These ruminations on the buying habits of the mass audience recall a talk I once had with a famous industrial designer whose work covered everything from designing gas stations to outdoor furniture. He admitted having produced some articles in bad taste which appealed to a wide public but added that once in a while, very seldom, he was able to design something that was right for everyone, that is to say an article, like a lamp, which would sell equally well in a quality shop or from a department store bargain counter. In other words, he'd occasionally come up with a fine design of universal appeal.

The saying "Plus ça change, plus c'est la même chose" has some application to certain phases of publishing, such as the editorial function. Enormous changes have taken place over the years, however. Indeed, the publisher of today is almost unrecognizable from his nineteenth-century predecessor. He was a law unto himself and he occupied a unique position. When, for example, John Murray of London published Byron's *Don Juan,* it caused the kind of sensation that a Hollywood preview of a great motion picture does today. The crowd in the street in front of Murray's office, clamoring for copies of *Don Juan* on publication date, was so dense and so obstreperous as to necessitate calling out the police!

57

In that era the book publisher possessed great power—too much. It is well known that after Byron had delivered the manuscript of his memoirs, John Murray was doubtful about the propriety of publishing them. He consulted some literary gentlemen of his acquaintance who came to the conclusion that they were in bad taste, were embarassingly frank, and should not be printed. Thereupon this priceless manuscript was consigned to the flames in Mr. Murray's office, to the great loss of succeeding generations.

Much later, in the first quarter of this century, when literary agents began to exert an influence, a well-known London publisher summoned one of his authors, a fine journalist and biographer. This man, A. G. Gardiner, told me that the publisher, a shrewd old gentleman, had heard that he, Gardiner, proposed to write a life of Christ. When the question of progress on the manuscript was raised, Gardiner admitted he had started the book and that the first part was in the hands of his agent. "Agent," screamed the publisher, "you mean to say you have employed an agent!" Then, as Gardiner mumbled his explanation, he noticed tears in the eyes of his publisher, who finally pulled himself together and exclaimed: "To think, Mr. Gardiner, that you should have dealt with an agent, particularly in a case involving the life of Our Saviour, is really more than I can bear."

By the time I had started work in the literary marketplace, publishers had recovered from the shock of relatively new inventions that absorbed the leisure hours of potential readers; but I heard many stories from the older bookmen about their earlier fears of the threat of the gramophone, the motion picture, and even the automobile. As the years passed, radio, followed by television, appeared on the scene and I admit that when the television sets proliferated, I began to fear for books which had survived so many technical innovations as well as the competition of the magazine fiction serial.

Today it is hard to judge the effect of television on book reading. Light fiction is harder to sell but the sale of children's books has increased more rapidly than that of any other publishing category except textbooks, an extraordinary development to all of us who have observed children glued to the television set for hours on end. Whatever is the answer to the question of the effects of television it is clear that, as education in its broadest sense has spread, so has the habit of reading for the public as a whole. Although the book "carriage trade" has largely disappeared, it has been replaced by other book buyers.

Important developments of the 20's and 30's were the start of book clubs and of paperbacks. In addition, the 20's, a period of intense literary activity, marked the appearance of a number of important new publishing houses as major factors in the industry—Alfred Knopf, Harcourt Brace, Random House, Simon & Schuster, Viking Press. They brought new energy and excitement to publishing. And they improved the format of books, finding, as well, more effective ways of advertising and promoting their product.

I don't think that anyone is quite certain as to who was the book-club pioneer—Harry Scherman, a former mail-order man, or Harold Guinzburg, the publisher-owner of the Viking Press. The Book-of-the-Month Club (Scherman) and the Literary Guild were started in the same year, 1926. These clubs aroused a furor in bookselling circles where it was felt that book-club price-cutting would adversely affect the traditional type of retail sales. Actually, the argument about book clubs persists to some extent, although most knowledgeable people now admit that club mail-order operations have created hundreds of thousands of new book-buyers in areas where booksellers are scarce or nonexistent. The fact is that Scherman and Guinzburg discovered a new way of selling books and succeeded in getting them into the hands of people who had never acquired the book-buying habit.

The other major development in the years preceding World War II was the beginning of the current American paperback. In 1939 Robert de Graff launched Pocket Books. They seemed a dangerous innovation to most of the clothbound publishers who had forgotten that paper books were widely sold in the nineteenth century until a price war ended this type of publishing for a long time. Some publishers refused to sell publication rights to de Graff but his enterprise throve so that, soon, other paperback firms were started.

The effect of paperbacks on publishing and on

reading habits has been enormous. These books, distributed throughout the country in tens of thousands of new book outlets, lured away a considerable part of the pulp magazine audience. Then, as paperbacks caught on, the clothbound publishers started their own lines, which were sold largely in the regular bookstores — books of a higher quality than those then put out by the mass publishers. In time, the mass paperback publishers added "quality lines" to their output. As a result of this paperback revolution, the number of book readers has greatly increased, college bookstores have developed impressively, and education has benefited from the appearance of many paperback editions of classics and of out-of-print books of high quality. Moreover, the sale of the paperbacks, which are mostly reprints of clothbound titles, has not measurably cut into the original publisher's sales as was feared. In some cases, even, the paperback edition has increased the clothbound sale of the same title, although this result is hardly typical.

Perhaps change seems more rapid when one has been recently experiencing it. At any rate the changes in publishing over the past fifteen years are striking. They affect all areas of book publishing, as might be expected, since the dividing lines between trade and educational books, between adult and children's books have become hazier.

The growth of textbook publishing has been phenomenal. Not only have the school and college populations grown rapidly but the number of books used, per student, has also increased. Beyond that,

61

Americans have become progressively more education conscious. Although the effect of a single event can be exaggerated, I believe that Sputnik, which took wing in 1957, was a turning point. It brought to people in this country the sudden realization that we were lagging in education, that in some fields we were behind the Russians. Americans at last took in the obvious truth that if the United States was to maintain a leading position in the world, more and better education was required. Sputnik was the shock needed to jolt us out of our smugness.

One of the most important — and favorable — developments, particularly for trade books, has been the increase in what we call institutional buying, that is, buying by libraries, schools and such organizations as the Armed Forces. Without this type of purchasing, accelerated by grants from the Federal government, trade publishers would have been in a bad way, having lost most of their "carriage trade." The fact that fifty per cent of Harper's adult trade books are now sold to institutions, and seventy-five per cent of our juveniles, is a measure of the importance of this source of demand.

Fifteen years ago the college store was apt to be a place where you bought banners, football shoes, fountain pens and, occasionally, a textbook when required to do so. With few exceptions, college stores carried no stock of general books except for a scattering of paperbacks. To visit this type of store in a big university center was a most depressing experience. Now, a new and brighter day has dawned for the college store, due in large part to paper-backs. For as an increasing number of works of distinction became available in paper at moderate prices these stores started to buy and stock them. This led, in certain cases, to purchases of cloth-bound titles other than textbooks. In consequence, while there is still plenty of room for improvement, the college store of today in many universities has achieved real stature and functions as an essential part of the educational system. Indeed some of them are impressive with their excellent representation of current titles which often include arresting displays of art books.

Among the most important developments of recent years is the increasing use of the general trade type of book in education. While this is of course welcome to the trade publisher, the implications are much greater in terms of education. Currently, the student in a superior college is exposed to the best books on any given subject, to supplement the basic texts. This emphasis has become more general in recent years and is spreading to the schools. To a considerable degree the development of excellent paperback lines has contributed to better education.

In considering the course of publishing over recent years the problem of salacious writing, pornographic books, is bound to arise. It raises the questions of censorship and of the publisher's responsibility.

My reaction to the problem is necessarily individualistic. While I believe that any kind of blanket censorship is both impractical and wrong, I feel that some books now published are books of no literary value, exploiting sex for its shock effect, and should not see the light of day. In making this statement I, of course, take into account the great change in sex mores since the last world war. And I'm fully aware that taste and standards vary enormously from period to period; witness the contrast between Restoration and Victorian attitudes. Yet there is some limit to what should appear in print for general distribution.

Looking back, the fact that Joyce's *Ulysses* was published in France many years before the book could be brought out here seems fantastic to us now. Also, the furor over *Lady Chatterley's Lover,* when it appeared, is hard for the present generation to believe. There are many examples of this sort, including that of *The Well of Loneliness,* in its time (1928) a shocker because it dealt candidly with Lesbianism.

Nabokov's *Lolita* seemed quite a shocker even in 1958. This is a book which I would have wanted to publish, had I been given the opportunity to read it in manuscript, because of its literary distinction and because the author described with wit and perhaps deliberate exaggeration a human situation that is not necessarily abnormal.

In contrast to this novel, however, there are many crudely written books, designed solely to produce a sensational effect, which appear in print. These are the ones that involve the difficult decisions.

64

Part of what I call the pornographic problem is that of pricing. A borderline book sold at $6.95 makes a different impact from one costing 75¢; the latter will reach a big group of teen-agers unable to afford the higher price. On theoretical grounds pricing makes no difference; from an ethical standpoint one cannot make distinctions in terms of price. But there is a practical difference in judging what might be harmful to a million people as against, say, twenty thousand relatively sophisticated readers. The difference is recognized by society in that there has always been more censorship of one kind or another in the mass media like motion pictures and television than in the media affecting a limited public. The pricing problem is a complicating factor in this whole swampy area.

Although reputable publishers can generally be trusted in the matter of pornographic books there will always be some attracted to making a fast buck. In this situation the question arises whether some kind of censorship is needed and, if so, what.

I distrust the pat answer to these questions from sources which have an interest in unlimited freedom of the press with no holds barred. Nevertheless, I am quite apprehensive about any kind of censorship, even though applied with restraint by the courts. As to censorship imposed by voluntary organizations like the Watch and Ward Society or by the police in various localities, I'm convinced that it must not be permitted. On the other hand I cannot avoid the conclusion that censorship by the courts may occasionally be necessary.

Let us imagine a hypothetical case — John Smith, a clever, tortuous type, determines to start a pornographic publication, partly for his own amusement, partly to make a quick profit. He produces one, say a magazine, the pictures and text of which express the most perverted, violent, and shocking view of human sexual behavior imaginable. Should this magazine, deliberately designed to corrupt, be widely available? I believe that most responsible citizens would say no. They would be apt to observe, "I don't believe in censorship, but ..."

I wish that I could express a more clear-cut view on censorship and pornography but there are no easy answers to the many questions that arise. The problem of restraining an excess of tolerance in this area is soluble only by the exercise of careful judgment in each individual case. Probably the basic, long-term solution is for parents and teachers to strive to educate the taste of children so that pornography will not hold their interest for long, to the exclusion of more rewarding books. Education is a long, hard road but eventually it gets somewhere — to a point of no return that is well worth all the effort.

What about the future of publishing? The answer depends on whether it is given by an optimist or a pessimist. As I see it, two opposing cultural trends are at work, one tending toward mechanical standardization, the other toward the stimulation of excellence through education.

Like fire, the machine can be a benefit or a disaster, depending upon the use that is made of it. That there exists today a tendency toward standardization is apparent; the mass media of communication give plenty of evidence of it. But this does not mean that the use of electronic devices in teaching must be a purely mechanical one nor that these devices cannot be adapted to individual needs, although I believe that education by electronics will, necessarily, be confined to certain teaching areas where factual presentations rather than intellectual concepts are involved.

Recently I have been interested in an electronic program for teaching science to schoolchildren, supplementing a series of textbooks published by my firm. I observed a boy of nine, one not specially trained, receiving instruction recorded on tape from a machine. The child was fascinated by the process and utterly concentrated in spite of the presence of a phalanx of kibitzing adults. I would have been fascinated too, had I been allowed to take his place. For the machine appeared to take a personal interest in this boy who was pressing the buttons. It told him when he was wrong, complimented him when he was right and, at the end, gave him a good idea as to whether the course was too easy or too difficult for him. Moreover, it was apparent that the tape recording would be useful to his teacher, since it graded the child's performance and eliminated the necessity for the teacher to go through this time-consuming process.

I admit the temptation to exaggerate the importance of a new teaching device because of its novelty, and so must make the obvious qualification that a machine is of value only to the extent that an excellent teaching program is fed into it. Nonetheless, I was impressed by the possibilities of the demonstration I attended and can see an important future for mechanical instruction in taking the place of the routine kind of teaching, provided that first-class intellects are involved in the preparation of the programs.

No doubt the role of the author in the academic field is going to change; he will be concerned, in the educational field, with creating programs as well as books. Without him the softwear, a term suggesting Macy's basement but used to describe these programs, could not be properly produced.

The problem of combining softwear with hardware has led to the acquisition of publishing concerns by big electronic companies. Mergers, such as those of Random House with R.C.A. and Holt, Rinehart with C.B.S., were designed to achieve a combination of editorial know-how and the technical facilities needed to provide what can be broadly described as the teaching machines. Actually, the merging process is not the only solution since, already, the great electronic concerns like R.C.A. are making arrangements with important, independently owned publishers for the use of their editorial material.

In a word, I believe that the publisher's function in the future will be fully as important as it is today. Techniques of conveying information will change and develop greatly, yet no one but the creative author can produce the required educational material and no one but the good editor can help him do so.

I believe that the publisher of the next generation will publish as many books as the publisher does today and on as many subjects, although some of the subjects may be new. For the book is not only a necessary source for teaching programs but also the best, and probably the only, tool where complicated subjects are involved. And, so far as the general public is concerned, the book offers a unique variety of stimulation and entertainment.

After many years in publishing, the question naturally arises whether the experience has been a satisfying one. My answer is yes, on the whole, with the qualification that the publisher can never be satisfied with his performance because, as in any difficult profession or craft, he is bound to be so conscious of the mistakes he has made. Yet I am happy to admit that my experience in publishing has been, and continues to be, intensely stimulating and absorbing. For, if a publisher is any good, he is bound to be in contact with the best minds of his time in almost every field; that is his job. So, he feels continually challenged—as is a player in a competitive sport—by being pitted against talent superior to his own.

On the minus side, there are very frequent discouraging moments. Many authors, because of their talent, are difficult to deal with; moreover, the publisher's work is full of detail, often tiresome. And, worst of all, the necessity of declining manuscript after manuscript, sometimes submitted by people you know and like, is extremely painful. Indeed, publishing is far from being a pleasure from beginning to end, although one never gets over the excitement of coming upon a good manuscript, especially by someone in whom you believe.

I suppose that the main satisfaction for an editor, like that of any craftsman, comes from knowing that occasionally he has done a good job on a particular book. There is satisfaction, also, when one has thought up an idea for a book that's needed and has found the right person to carry it out. When the editor achieves this he has fulfilled his need to express certain ideas and attitudes. He does this by finding talented individuals with a gift of expression which he himself lacks.

The difficulty of trying to describe the characteristics of the good editor-publisher is formidable. He appears to me to be part chameleon, part hummingbird tasting every literary flower, and part warrior-ant. I would emphasize the chameleon aspect because the editor must change his color to reflect changing attitudes and tastes. Unless he is at all stages of his career the product of the moment with his eyes on the future, he will succumb to his more alert competitors. He cannot rest, nor will he want to, so long as he can practice the sometimes frustrating but always exciting, ever-changing and challenging occupation of publishing books.

70

AFTERWORD

CONVERSATION WITH LEON TROTSKY ON FEBRUARY 4, 1940

(These notes were made at the time of the author's visit to Trotsky's house in Mexico City. His observations and prophecies are of interest in view of the fact that the interview took place about four months before the Nazi invasion of the Lowlands and France, and sixteen months before Hitler's invasion of Russia.)

Trotsky gave the impression, in terms of vitality of health, of a man of forty; actually he was sixty-three years old in 1940. I was struck by his fine brow and shock of white hair — his strong face and expressive mouth. He was well dressed in gray trousers and a white Russian smock.

Trotsky complained of the difficulty of obtaining source material for his book in Mexico and alluded to the problem of obtaining — anywhere — authentic facts about Stalin.

I asked him about the situation in Europe in early 1940. In reply he said that the failure of the Soviet offensive against the Finns was no surprise to him. He pointed out that the Soviet officers were watched by commissars and were fearful of them. And he added that it would take Russia a long time to recover from two purges, first that of the aristocracy and bourgeoisie in the Revolution, and second, the purge of ability effected by Stalin. However, Trotsky stated that there was no question in his mind that the Russians would finally achieve a breakthrough in Finland.

He made the observation that the Communist Party no longer ruled in Russia. Trotsky called it a rubber stamp for the bureaucracy and compared the Party to the Nazi setup in Germany.

Trotsky summarized the sequence of events in Europe. He said that England had armed Hitler by selling him the supplies he needed; that Hitler then succeeded in keeping England friendly or at least not openly hostile while he took territory of military and industrial value — Austria and Czechoslovakia. Having done this and incurred British hostility, Hitler proceeded to make the pact with Stalin, who had been eager for some time to establish friendly relations. Trotsky pictured Stalin as a shrewd tactician ready to make any deal to tide over immediate danger. He expressed the opinion that Stalin did not expect Hitler to win the war and would, at the right moment, desert him, having in the meantime escaped attack and acquired territory.

Trotsky expressed admiration for Hitler as a master strategist. He stated that in his view the German economy, the most dynamic in the world, *had* to expand. He thought that although one might consider that Hitler made a mistake in bringing on war he, Hitler, had no choice because Germany was bound for economic disaster without further expansion.

Trotsky stated his belief that Germany would lose the war but only after a terrific struggle, since

72

Russia would be valuable as a source of supply. He said that America would have to become a belligerent in order to save the Allies.

At this point Trotsky exclaimed: "And then what? A ruined planet under the hegemony of the United States. Revolution in the United States and elsewhere, creating chaos and suffering because it would come at a time of profound economic dislocation." Trotsky expressed the opinion that the British Empire was coming to an end and that the colonies would split off soon. He felt that Britain had shown her lack of vitality by her policy of appeasement which culminated at Munich.

At the end of the conversation I asked Trotsky whether he still wanted to enter the United States, to which he replied: "Most certainly. And if it were not for 'that man in the White House' I would be there now." In explanation, he added that F.D.R. was a liberal and knew too much about him whereas a Republican president might have let him in.

Finally I asked him: "What would you do if you could get into the United States?" Answer: "Start a revolution, of course."